little hands
FRUIT

RACHEL MATTHEWS

Chrysalis Children's Books

Fruit grows on trees, bushes and plants.

A fruit is the part of a plant that contains seeds.

Collect some
different fruits.

How many
colours can
you find?

What does each fruit feel like?

spiky

waxy

furry

hairy

bumpy

rough

smooth

firm

Many fruits look and feel different on the inside.

grapefruit

apricot

kiwi

apple

lime

papaya

cherry

orange

Look inside some fruits.
What differences do you notice?

Some fruits have lots of small seeds inside.

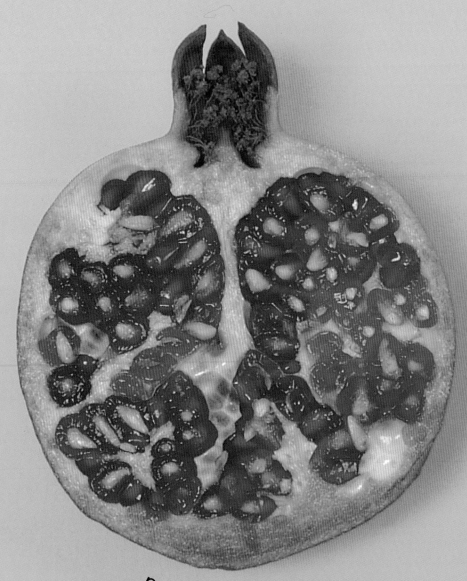

pomegranate

Others just have one large seed.

peach

What happens when you plant a fruit seed?

Over time, it can grow into a big fruit tree.

Try eating some different fruits. Smell each one first.

Do you need to take off the outer layer?

What does it feel like when you bite into it?

Most fruits
taste sweet.
A lemon
tastes sour!

You can squeeze juice from some fruits.

How can you tell when a fruit is ready to eat?
Some fruits change colour as they ripen.

Some fruits become soft when they are ripe.

Other fruits smell stronger. They taste sweeter, too.

mangoes

Fruits are the food of many animals.
Chimps like munching mangoes.

18

There are even fruit-eating fish!

Some fruits taste good when they are dried.
Which of these dried fruits have you tried?

fig

papaya

pineapple

dates

apple

raisins (grapes)

banana

apricot

pear

We can cook with fruits.

Make a
fruit salad.
What's your
favourite fruit?

Notes for teachers and parents

Pages 2–3
The fruit is the part of a plant that contains seeds, so cucumbers, peppers, pea pods and tomatoes are all fruits.
Discussion: Encourage the children to tell you what they know about fruit; which fruits do they eat at school and at home? What fruit flavourings are used in desserts, sweets and ice creams? Have they used fruit-scented soap or shampoo?
Activity: Take the children to visit a pick-your-own farm so that they can see fruit growing on trees and bushes. Bring back produce and set up your own fruit stall. This could promote the importance of eating fruit as part of a healthy diet.

Pages 4–7
Activity: Buy some fruit from a supermarket labelled with each country of origin. On a map, show the children how far each fruit has travelled and how much (or how little) fruit is grown locally.
Discussion: Encourage the children to name and describe each piece of fruit and explain how it differs in colour, size, shape and texture from another, eg. "This is a banana. It's long, smooth and yellow. This tomato is smaller and it's round, shiny and red."
Activity: Cut open the fruits and ask the children to describe the difference between the interior and exterior. Use specialized vocabulary such as skin, rind, stalk, flesh and juice.

Pages 8–9
Activity: Collect and count seeds from a fruit. Large quantities of seeds (such as from a melon or pumpkin) could be counted into groups of ten. The children could make their own seed packets with drawings of the fruits from which they were obtained.

Pages 10–11
Growing plants from seeds allows children to explore the conditions necessary for germination.
Experiment: Set up parallel experiments, planting seeds in two pots and leaving the soil in one pot unwatered, so that the children can compare the results. Once the children have seen seedlings appear, you could bring in a plant (grown at home or bought from a garden centre) at a later stage in its life cycle.
Activity: If you have a garden, you could grow fruiting plants such as strawberries and tomatoes, so the children can watch the flowers and fruits develop.

Pages 12–15
Discussion: Ask the children which fruits have the strongest scents. Which scents do they like best?
Discussion: Encourage the children to describe the taste and texture of each fruit and compare it to others, eg. "An apple is crunchy and juicy and it tastes a bit sharp. This peach is softer and more juicy and it tastes sweeter."

Pages 16–19
Fruit ripens as the seeds it contains become ready to be dispersed. Unripe fruit tastes unpleasant, so animals in the wild will wait until the fruit is ripe before eating it. Seeds are dispersed as they travel through the animals' bodies intact.
Experiment: Show the children some hard green bananas and photograph them every day as they ripen and rot to provide a visual record of the whole process.

Pages 20–21
Experiment: Provide a selection of fresh fruits and their dried equivalents. Can the children match up the fresh and dried fruit? Taking account of any allergies, let the children taste the fresh and dried versions. What similarities and differences are there?
Activity: If you have cooking facilities, make a fruit cake or pie with the children and let them taste the finished product. Talk about how fruits change when they are cooked.

Page 22
Activity: Make a fruit salad for everyone to share. Display the recipe with the children's paintings of fruit.

Index

First published in the UK in 2005 by
Chrysalis Children's Books
An imprint of Chrysalis Books Group Plc
The Chrysalis Building, Bramley Road
London W10 6SP

Copyright © Chrysalis Books Group Plc 2005

All rights reserved.

ISBN 1 84458 176 4

British Library Cataloguing in Publication Data for this book is available
from the British Library.

Associate publisher *Joyce Bentley*
Project manager and editor *Penny Worm*
Art director *Sarah Goodwin*
Designer *Patricia Hopkins*
Picture researchers *Veneta Bullen, Miguel Lamas*
Photographer *Ray Moller*

The author and publishers would like to thank the following people for their
contributions to this book: Ruth Thomson, Mollie Worms and Mollie Parker.

Printed in China

10 9 8 7 6 5 4 3 2 1

Typography *Natascha Frensch*

Read Regular, READ SMALLCAPS and Read Space; European Community
Design Registration 2003 and Copyright © Natascha Frensch 2001-2004
Read Medium, **Read Black** and *Read Slanted* Copyright © Natascha Frensch
2003-2004

READ™ is a revolutionary new typeface that will enhance children's understanding
through clear, easily recognisable character shapes. With its evenly spaced and
carefully designed characters, READ™ will help children at all stages to improve
their literacy skills, and is ideal for young readers, reluctant readers and especially
children with dyslexia.

Picture acknowledgements
All reasonable efforts have been made to ensure the reproduction of content
has been done with the consent of copyright owner. If you are aware of any
unintentional omissions please contact the publishers directly so that any
necessary corrections may be made for future editions.
Getty Images: Peter Lilja 18; Papilio: Robert Pickett 19.